Trails, Tails & Tidepools in Pails

D1515035

Published by Nursery Nature Walks
1440 Harvard Street
Santa Monica, CA 90404

First Edition 1992

Second Edition 1994 revised

Library of Congress Cataloging in Publication Data

Nursery Nature Walks
Trails, Tails & Tidepools in Pails
        Over 100 Fun and Easy Nature Activities
        for Families and Teachers to Share
        with Babies and Young Children

by the Docents of Nursery Nature Walks

2nd edition revised includes subject and age-appropriate index
1. Activity programs
2. Child rearing
3. Environmental education
        A. Conservation
        B. Teaching and studying
4. Nature study
5. Parenting

Library of Congress card number 94-65875

ISBN 0-9632753-1-3, 2nd edition, $9.95 softcover
ISBN 0-9632753-0-5, 1st edition, $9.95 softcover

Trails, Tails & Tidepools in Pails

Over 100 Fun and Easy Nature Activities
for Families and Teachers to Share
with Babies and Young Children

by the Docents of Nursery Nature Walks
illustrated by Marlena Day

ACKNOWLEDGEMENTS

This book was created with love and laughter. It grew, changed and blossomed over three years. DeAnn Rushall, one of the original docents, was the source of the majority of the activities. Other Nursery Nature Walks docents also contributed their ideas. Bernadette Laqueur and Lisa Delucci compiled activities during the first year. Joli Jacobs, Debbie Aaberg and Judy Burns were the primary authors. Debbie compiled and structured the activities and pages, then Joli transposed them into her whimsical style and Judy supervised and edited. Marlena Day designed, typeset and illustrated all the pages. Throughout this process the docents of NNW continued to test and refine the various activities.

Nursery Nature Walks wishes to thank Harriet Bennish, NNW Founder; Jean Dillingham, Charisse Burdick, Tom Brown, Jr., and Marci Cohen for contributing activity ideas; Debbie Aaberg for indexing the activities; Linda Bodek for researching, planning and organizing the book publishing, distribution and marketing; Milt McAuley for publishing and marketing assistance; Susan Bernard for helping with fund-raising and marketing; our technical proofreaders Kimball Garrett, Los Angeles Natural History Museum; Ruth Lebow, geological engineer; Valerie Vartanian, naturalist; and Milt McAuley, author of numerous guidebooks to the Santa Monica Mountains; Jean Aaberg, Sue Depsky, Bernadette Laqueur and Marilyn Novell, who proofed the final document; and Jean Berlfein, Vivian Chen, Suzanne Dahlin, Anna Marie Daniels, Sue Depsky, Karren Gratt, Barbara Harrison, Susan Hodgson, Gene Marsh, Sue Othmer and Kay Sanger for their contributions. We especially thank our docents and our walkers for their continuous inspiration and creativity.

The printing of this book was made possible
through a generous donation from

the Landon family
in loving memory of Michael Landon

Nursery Nature Walks is a nonprofit environmental organization run by volunteers and supported by donations. All profits from this book will help support NNW programs, including walks for disadvantaged children.

Nursery Nature Walks was organized in 1985 when eighteen volunteers were trained to lead nature walks at five sites. Today our volunteers provide nature programs for thousands of families a year in Southern California. NNW also trains community leaders and provides programs for disadvantaged children. We host an annual nature festival, educate through publications and are working on making this model program nationally replicable.

Our mission is to educate parents, young children and educators about the fragility of nature, the joy in its exploration and the need to protect our wilderness and wildlife areas. We believe that this can be accomplished in parklands or around a sidewalk crack, all while providing opportunities for joyfully shared family time.

A fundamental message that Nursery Nature Walks volunteers teach is respect. We believe that the development of respect in children is essential for the preservation and appreciation of our wilderness and wildlife, and for the tranquility and well-being of our urban society. Our children must learn how to protect and respect the world in which they live.

To order a book send $9.95 plus $2.50 shipping and handling. California residents add applicable tax.

Nursery Nature Walks
1440 Harvard Street
Santa Monica, CA 90404

(310) 998-1161
or
(1-800) 597-6799

The activities in this book are very simple; most require few materials. For some you will only need a windy day or a tree.

Our hope is to offer ideas that can help families find the simplicity of enjoying nature. We want adults to look at nature through the eyes of their children. This is why our pages address the child and are meant to be read aloud (with the exception of activities for babies). These experiences leave room for the child's own interpretation, imagination and improvisation. Each time you pick out an activity, you and your child will discover something new. You can add to the ideas or even change them depending on your surroundings.

Our age range recommendations, listed with each activity, are just that—recommendations. These are the ages we've had the most success with when it comes to each adventure. By all means use your own judgment. All kids develop at different rates.

It's not necessary to travel far to find a nature trail. Your backyard or a sidewalk crack have just as many bustling bugs and blooming buds as do the local hills and mountains.

The underlying message throughout this book is LET NATURE BE. Pick up a rock, put it back; turn over a log, replace it again; collect a bag of leaves, free them before you travel on; befriend a grasshopper, let it hop home.

We hope adults will carry this message to their children. We feel this is the key to teaching our youngsters that the environment must be respected and nurtured; that every pod, flower and insect has a purpose just where it is found. Children who respect the world around them are also learning to respect families and each other.

Enjoy and let it be!

CAUTIONS

This page was not written to scare you out of stepping into nature with kids. There are not dangers lurking around every bend and behind every tree. We have just jotted down the safety recommendations we use to help us carry out tear-free nature walks.

Some of our tips are quite obvious, others are not. Keep them in mind and everyone will come home with a smile.

HIKING GARB—We like to wear long, loose pants, closed-toe shoes and hats. Unless it's 100°F outside, we also wear long-sleeved shirts. These clothes are protection against sunburn, cold chills, stings, bites, scratches and rashes. Also, don't forget sun protection!

BRING WATER—When kids get thirsty, they can become quite irritable-so can adults for that matter. If you forget your canteen, it's not wise to drink water out of ponds, streams, lakes, etc., even if the water looks clear. It's not for fear of getting tadpoles stuck in your teeth-it's for fear of contamination. Most untreated water has some form of contaminants.

DITCH THE STICKS—Kids love sticks-the bigger the better. Picking up a stick is fine, but walking and running with it can be a little precarious. Bumps and ditches are easy to trip over, and tripping on a stick is no fun. We recommend no sticks on the trail.

DON'T EAT THE PLANTS—It is not recommended to eat plants along a trail. Many edible plants closely resemble non-edible ones. Unless you are an expert, it is very difficult to know the difference. Even plants that are "edible" can be toxic during some seasons or without proper preparation. Small children and some adults may have allergic reactions to wild foods.

STAY ON THE TRAIL—Try not to stray off a marked trail or path. Bush-whacking may seem fun, but it's not safe for you or for the plants and animals you're tromping over. A little foot might land on top of a startled animal or in the middle of a poison oak patch.

WATCH YOUR HANDS AND FEET—Keep hands out of holes. Holes are often homes for animals, including snakes. Little fleas can also live around the hole entrances waiting to hop on some furry critter. Some fleas carry disease.

In general, don't put your hands where you can't see. Check an area before children are allowed to explore.

LEAVES OF THREE, LET IT BE—The most common three-leaved plants are poison oak or ivy. Their leaves vary in color, size and shape. If you are unfamiliar with poison oak or ivy and you see a three-leaved plant, avoid touching it so you don't develop an itchy rash.

STAY CLOSE TO YOUR KIDS—Young children should always stay near an adult on wilderness outings. We suggest one adult for every mobile child under the age of three years.

CONTENTS

SENSES

BIRDS, INSECTS AND OTHER ANIMALS

TREES AND PLANTS

LEAVING NATURE BEHIND

WHAT CAN YOU TAKE HOME?

Remember that new pals like pill bugs, spiders, flowers, tadpoles, frogs and trees are at home where you find them.

Imagine how it would feel if someone visited your home then decided they liked you so much they were going to take you away to live with them.

What would you miss?

You would probably miss your mom and dad, brothers and sisters, your bed, your toys, even your refrigerator. What else would you miss?

It's important to leave your friends behind. They love their homes just like you love yours!

Think of ways to make it easier to say goodbye to your nature friends. Here are some ideas ...

Pick up some stickers and/or rubber stamps of plants and animals you usually see along a trail.

> If you find a grasshopper and you have a grasshopper sticker, place the sticker in your hand. Later, if you see a rabbit and you have a rabbit stamp, stamp a rabbit on your wrist. At the end of your walk, you will have memories of all the friends you met. (If you don't have stamps or stickers, you can draw your friends on paper and carry your pictures home.)

Bring along squirt bottles or canteens filled with water.

> Instead of picking flowers, say hello by giving them a squirt. Leave plant friends behind with a drink of water.

Bring along small animal puppets or stuffed animals.

> You can take these animals for a walk, and bring them home with you again.

Take home nature sounds.

> Chirp with the birds, whistle with the wind, crunch like the leaves and bring these sounds home with you.

Carry a few clear small containers with air holes.

> You can gently scoop a bug into a container long enough to say hello and look at it closely. Say thank you and let the bug go. Watch it walk or fly back to its house.

Carry non-living treasures like pine cones, pebbles, rocks and acorns with you for a while, then find special places along the path to leave them behind.

NUZZLE NATURE

MATERIALS

Trees, leaves, etc.

AGES

Babies and up

BABIES LEARN BY TOUCHING

Hold your baby up to a plant, tree or stem of leaves.

Help her reach out to touch the tree's trunk, the stem or the petal.

Enjoy each bulge, crevice or slippery surface of the plant together.

Encourage your baby to learn with her whole body.

Each surface will feel different to her as it is brushed with the palm, pinkie, cheek, chin, nose, toes, thumb or knee.

Stroke, poke, tap and slide ... nuzzle.

Pick a branch and let her watch how it springs back.

Let your baby listen as you snap a twig in half.

Create a mobile in motion.

Lift fallen leaves from the ground and let them flutter back down in front of your child.

SNIFFS AND WHIFFS

COLLECT THE SMELLS ALONG YOUR PATH

Pack a few small empty bottles into your pockets and pouches.

Sniff the air.

Can you catch a smell?

Grab a handful of damp earth and stuff it into one bottle.

Pluck a few flower petals and drop them into another bottle.

Dunk a bottle into a stream or pond.

Can you find anything else for your bottles?

Peeled bark, crunched leaves and crushed grasses have smells too.

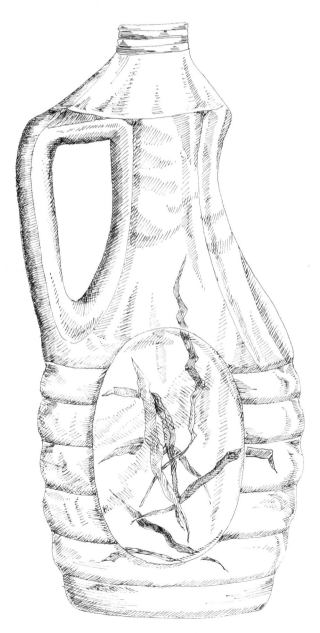

Line your bottles up and sniff them one at a time.

If you close your eyes, can you tell what you are smelling?

FEELING THE EARTH

MATERIALS

Soil

AGES

Babies and all ages

DIG YOUR HANDS AND TOES INTO THE EARTH!

There can be all sorts of different kinds of soil and earth in a small area. Did you know that the sand on each beach or that each plot of earth feels unique?

Walk along and dig.

Look for rocky earth, sandy earth, muddy earth, clay earth, soft damp leafy earth and hard dry cracked earth.

If you want, you can collect your earthy samples in small paper cups or paper plates.

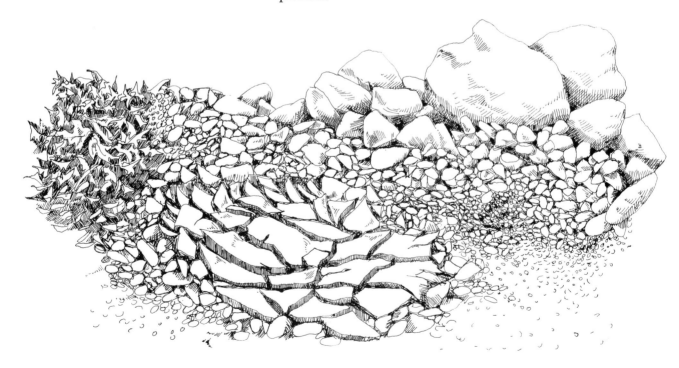

Feel the different samples with your fingers, hands, toes, elbows and knees.

It's easy for tiny babies to feel the difference in earth samples because their skin is so sensitive.

Put a little water into the paper cups and feel them again.

CAN MOMS, DADS, BROTHERS AND SISTERS FEEL THE DIFFERENCE TOO?

EYE AND EAR HELPERS

MATERIALS

Paper towel or toilet
   paper rolls
Paper
Tape
String or yarn

AGES

Toddlers
Preschoolers

ANOTHER IDEA

If you can locate them,
cardboard or plastic
industrial thread spools
make great eye and ear
helpers too!

TURN EMPTY PAPER ROLLS INTO EYE AND EAR HELPERS

Cover a paper roll with colored paper. Leave the ends of the tube open. Secure the paper with tape.

Poke a hole at one end of one side of the roll. Thread some string through the hole and make a necklace-sized loop. Tie off the loop with a knot.

(Parents or adult friends will need to help with construction!)

WEAR YOUR EYE AND EAR HELPER AROUND YOUR NECK AS YOU WALK

Spot a bright flower or tree.

You can see it with your eyes, now try to peek at it through your paper roll.

Use your eye helper like a telescope to look at nature friends like bugs, leaves, trees and rocks.

If you can, get up real close to your friends to peek at them through the telescope. Do they look bigger?

Place your hand in front of the hole at the end of your telescope, then take your hand away and play "peek-a-boo!" with your nature friends.

Turn the eye helper into an ear helper by placing the paper roll up to your ear.

Can you hear birds singing, or wind blowing, or water splashing or crickets chirping?

Keep listening for special sounds. What can you hear through your ear helper now?

MATCH-A-BATCH OF COLORS

MATERIALS

Colored construction
   paper
Scissors

Optional: For durability's
sake, color cards can be
laminated by covering them
with clear contact paper.

AGES

Toddlers
Preschoolers

HAND YOUR CHILD A SPLASH OF NATURE'S COLOR

Snip squares or circles out of a variety of colored construction paper.

Make sure that your shapes are large
enough for little hands to hold on to!

Let your child choose a color that catches
her eye.

FREE HANDS!

If your child has a rough
time holding on to her color
card, a piece of string or yarn
will turn it into a necklace.

Discover the color in trees, flowers, fallen leaves, rocks, feathers ... whatever may be waiting along your path.

Verbally repeat the color when your child finds its match in nature.

Choose a new color after a bit, and continue your matching adventure.

SOUNDS OF SILENCE

MATERIALS

The sounds of nature

AGES

Toddlers
Preschoolers

GIVING THANKS

American Indians had a very deep appreciation for the natural world around them. Indian children learned very early to give thanks to nature for providing shelter and food.

DEER EARS

Stop quietly along the trail.

Cup your hands behind your ears.

Notice that everything sounds louder and clearer. Deer have large ears that are sensitive to sound. Indians learned to imitate these ears to sharpen their own hearing.

Listen to the beautiful sounds of nature.

Hear the birds singing. How many different sounds can you hear?

Listen for the leaves rustling in the wind, or the sounds of a running stream.

Can you hear a squirrel chirping in the trees? Or the bees buzzing? Or the frogs croaking?

FOX WALKING

Put one foot quietly in front of the other and walk like a fox.

You might even surprise a cottontail rabbit or a ground squirrel as you silently observe the world around you.

Thanks to Tom Brown, Jr., for introducing us to "Deer Ears" and "Fox Walking."

SOUNDS OF NIGHT

MATERIALS

Your ears

AGES

Toddlers
Preschoolers

WHO'S AWAKE WHILE YOU'RE ASLEEP?

Perk up your ears, close your eyes and listen to the different sounds of night.

In the city, night sounds you commonly hear are cars beeping, sirens shrieking and people talking.

Late at night, when things are quiet, you can listen for crickets chirping, owls hooting, cats meowing, dogs barking and wind whooshing.

In the woods at night, you can listen for many animal sounds.

Pretend you are a night animal.

HOWL like a coyote.

YAP like a fox.

SNIFF like a raccoon.

RUSTLE like a deer.

SCAMPER like a mouse.

HOOT like an owl.

SQUEAK like a bat.

CHIRP like a cricket.

CALLING ALL BIRDS

AGES

Toddlers and up

KISS THE BACK OF YOUR HAND TO MAKE SQUEAKY BIRD CALLS

Try to call the birds down from the trees and sky.

If you see a bird land next to you, stand quiet and still. How long can you make it stay before it flies away?

MORE BIRD CALLS

If kissing doesn't work, try "pishing." Softly make a "psshhh-psshhh-psshhh" sound.

IMITATE THE SONGS OF BIRDS.

Caw Caw like a crow.

Ork Ork like a raven.

Chi-ca-go like a quail.

Quack Quack like a duck.

*Coo Coo, wh-who-whoo
like a dove*

Hoo Hooo like an owl.

FEATHERED FLIGHTS AND FOOTWORK

AGES

Toddlers
Preschoolers

HOP AND WALK

Hop and walk like a bird.

Some birds that live on the ground walk like we do. Birds that live in trees hop on both feet when they're on the ground.

Hop like a tree bird, walk like a ground bird. Hop and walk, hop and walk.

Are you a tree bird or a ground bird?

BECOME A BIRD

Flap your wings as fast as you can like a hummingbird.

CAN BIRDS FLY BACKWARDS?

Hummingbirds are the only birds that fly backwards. They do this as they search for nectar among flowers. Hummingbirds eat about 50 meals of insects and nectar a day.

Swoop and squawk like a jay.

Bob your head like a walking
pigeon.

Peck like a hungry woodpecker
looking for insects.

Raise your arms into a wide V
and tilt from side to side like a
turkey vulture.

Soar high with the wind like a
hawk.

Lean forward and run like a
roadrunner.

Scratch the dirt with your feet
like a towhee hunting for
insects.

FEATHER FINDERS

MATERIALS

Feathers, three or more

AGES

All ages

START A COLLECTION OF FEATHERS

Pluck feathers off trails and paths as you walk together.

> They're easy to find. Look along the beach, or under trees or by ponds and streams. Sometimes you can even spot them floating in the air!

Sort through your collection.

Notice that some almost look alike and others look very different.

> How many colors and patterns can you find in your feathers?
> Are some fluffy and others stiff and smooth?
> Do they tickle when you run them up your arm or under your chin?

Try to find a short, fluffy, fine feather in your collection.

Feathers like these are called down feathers. Down lies underneath a bird's longer, more sturdy feathers. It keeps a bird warm and snug like a blanket.

Find a longer, stiffer feather in your collection.

Feathers like these are often wing feathers used for flying.

Run your fingers up and down a wing feather and watch how the feather separates in one direction, and "zips" together in the other.

Birds can use their beaks to close or zip their feathers. This way feathers catch the wind to help the bird fly high.

Free the feathers in your collection.

Chase them, blow them, then catch them again.

NEST BUILDERS

MATERIALS

Clay or playdough

AGES

Toddlers and up

IMITATE A NEST-BUILDING BIRD

If you've ever noticed a bird swooping by with a twig or stick in its beak, you've seen a nest-building bird.

Can you build a nest from the things you find along a trail?

Birds make nests from small twigs and dry grasses that lie on the ground. They also use fallen leaves, pine needles, bits of bark, feathers, even animal fur!

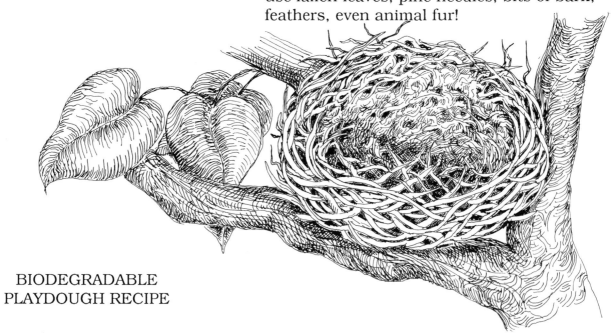

BIODEGRADABLE PLAYDOUGH RECIPE

1 cup flour
1/2 cup salt
2 tsp. cream of tartar
1 cup water
A few drops food coloring
1 tbs. salad oil

Mix all ingredients in skillet. Heat on low until lumpy. Stir occasionally. Put dough on waxed paper and knead until it cools.

Roll a piece of clay or playdough into a ball about the size of your palm to start your nest.

Stick your thumb in the center of the clay ball to turn it into a cup or nest shape.

*Now, as you walk, look for things that
you think would make a comfy nest
for tiny baby birds.*

*Push the things you find into your
clay nest.*

You can keep adding to your nest until you
feel it is ready for a baby bird to live in.

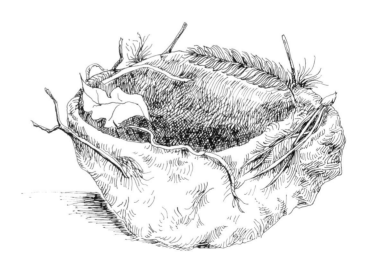

Place your nest in your yard.

See if a bird comes and decides to use any
part of your nest for its own.

WATER BIRD COATS

MATERIALS

Mineral oil or Vaseline
Spray bottle filled with
    water
Feathers

AGES

Toddlers
Preschoolers

DISCOVER HOW WATER BIRDS STAY WARM AND DRY

Rub mineral oil or Vaseline on your hand or arm.

Spritz the oil-covered area with water.

Watch the water form droplets and roll off your skin.

HOW DO BIRDS FLOAT?

Water birds cannot float without oil on their feathers, so they have special oil glands located near their tails. Until their own oil glands start working, baby birds get this oil from their mother's feathers as she sits with them in the nest.

Water birds such as ducks, pelicans and seagulls use their beaks to coat their feathers with oil. This oil keeps water birds dry and warm. Instead of soaking into feathers, water can form into droplets that easily roll off the birds' bodies.

Spritz water on the hand or arm that has not been protected by oil.

Notice how the water doesn't drop off this hand or arm as easily.

Lightly spray water on a feather.

What happens?

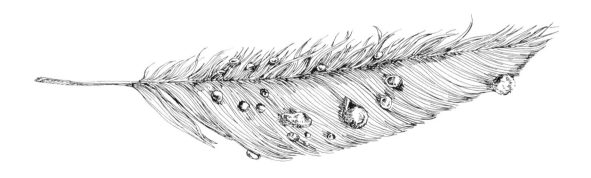

F L U T T E R S A N D M A R C H E S

AGES

Toddlers
Preschoolers

FLUTTER BY WITH A BUTTERFLY

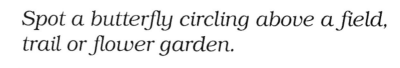

Spot a butterfly circling above a field, trail or flower garden.

Stretch out your arms and try to follow your fluttering friend.

Flutter up and down like a roller coaster.

Swoop and skip from one place to another.

Zig and zag back and forth along the path.

BUSY ANTS

Land and rest with your arm wings folded up above your head.

Ants live in colonies. The queen ant produces new ants including workers with specific jobs. Some feed the queen, some take care of the young ants, while others defend the colony from enemies. The ants you imitated are in charge of finding food.

Catch your breath, then take off again!

MARCH AND DANCE WITH A TRAIL OF ANTS

Step up to the trunk of a tree.

See if you can spot a trail of busy ants marching up and down the tree's bark.

Keep your eyes open wide as you wander along a path or trail.

Look for ants marching along the ground and see what they are carrying with them.

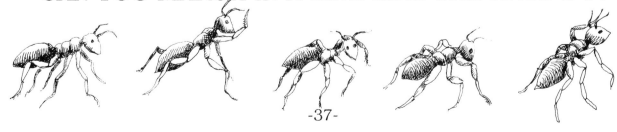

CAN YOU MARCH IN A LINE LIKE THE ANTS DO?

LADYBUG BALLET

MATERIALS

A ladybug beetle

AGES

Babies and up

FIND A LADYBUG BEETLE

Gently pluck a ladybug beetle off a leaf or flower.

You can often find them munching aphids on sweet fennel or rose petals.

Allow the ladybug to dance and travel around your palm or up your arm.

Take care! Ladybugs need to be held very softly.

LADYBUG FACTS

Ladybugs are one of the most commonly recognized beetles. Their bright color warns birds and reptiles that this beetle is not good to eat. It is considered very good luck to have ladybugs in your garden. They will help protect your garden from aphids. Technically the correct name for "ladybug" is ladybird beetle.

Notice that some ladybugs are plain red or plain orange while others have spots.

What does yours look like?

Clap as the ladybug flies away.

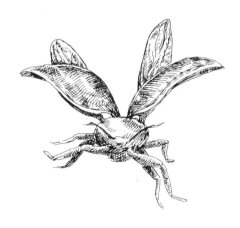

ADOPT A PILL BUG

MATERIALS

Pill bug or sow bug

AGES

Babies with help
Toddlers and up

BORROW A PILL BUG OR A SOW BUG

Simply turn over a rock or a piece of wood.

> Pill bugs always choose dark, damp places for their homes.

Gently pick up the pill bug.

Let it explore your hand.

> It is a gentle, harmless creature. Hold it carefully and let it crawl on your arm.

Enjoy the tickly sensation!

Return your little friend to his home.

> Even pill bugs have friends and families! Leave his home as you found it!

PILL BUG OR SOW BUG?

Pill bugs and sow bugs are members of the crustacean family. They are related to crabs and lobsters. You can tell the difference between the two because pill bugs roll into a little ball to protect themselves and sow bugs do not. Sow bugs are flat and can escape quickly underneath rocks and leaves.

PILL BUG WAKE-UP CHANT

If the pill bug rolls into a little ball, encourage him to open up by softly chanting:

> Wake up, wake up Mister Pill Bug
> Wake up, wake up Mister Pill Bug
> Wake up, wake up Mister Pill Bug

You can also try gently blowing on him until he uncurls.

WEB ART

MATERIALS

Spray bottle filled with
   water
Spider web

AGES

Toddlers
Preschoolers

SPIDER WEB ICICLES

Spot a spider web.

Spiders like grassy areas, shrubs and small branches to make their shiny homes.

Spray it once or twice with a gentle mist of water.

Please be careful not to drench the spider in its web!

Watch the web shimmer in the sun.

It looks as if icicles are hanging from its delicate strings.

HERE ARE SOME COMMON TYPES OF SPIDER WEBS.

ORB WEBS have a somewhat circular pattern and are usually found strung between twigs and small branches.

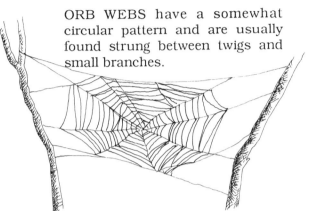

FUNNEL WEBS are often found in grassy areas and on shrubs. You can see the spider waiting for its prey in the hole at the base of the funnel.

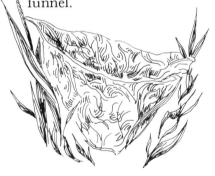

SHEET WEBS are irregularly shaped with threads extending in all directions. They are often found on shrubs.

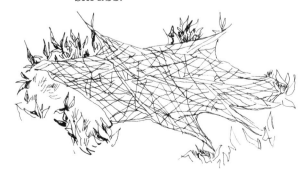

Serenade your new friend!

Your child will have lots of fun singing this old-time favorite.

"The itsey bitsey spider crawled up the water spout,

Down came the rain and washed the spider out,

Out came the sun and dried up all the rain,

And the itsey bitsey spider crawled up the spout again."

CRICKET CALLS

MATERIALS

Blindfolds
Children and adults
  (one adult per child)
One or more adult
  leaders

(This activity can be done
with many or few people)

AGES

Toddlers and up

CHIRP, CHIRP!
PRETEND YOU ARE A CRICKET

Have you ever tried to chirp without using your voice?
Well, crickets can!
Crickets don't have voices, but they can rub their wings together very fast and create high-sounding chirp sounds.

Imagine you are crickets in a huge field of tall grass and you need to find each other.

Adults can be the parent crickets, and children the baby crickets.

Think of a way you can call out to each other without using your voices.

How about clicking your tongues, tapping rocks together or clapping?

Agree upon one sound everyone can make. This will be the special cricket call.

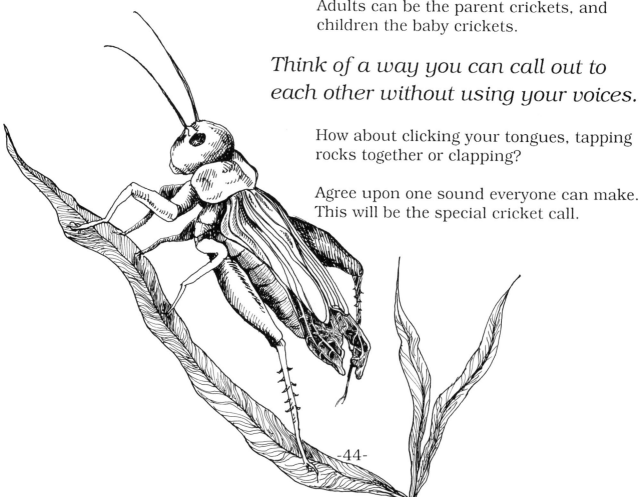

Blindfold the parent crickets and spin them around.

The leader's job is to guide the blindfolded crickets several yards away from the little crickets. Then the leader can signal baby crickets to start calling out to adults using the special sound.

See how long it takes for the parent crickets to find their little crickets as they walk toward the calling sound.

The leader can make sure blindfolded crickets don't get lost or hurt along the way!

WOULD YOU LIKE TO BE A CRICKET?

SNAIL TRAILS

MATERIALS

Several snails
Black construction
    paper

AGES

Babies and toddlers
    with help

Preschoolers and up

DISCOVER A SNAIL'S SILVER TRAIL

Follow its shimmering path across leaves of ivy, on top of dark green grass, over patches of dirt, or even up a wall!

SNAIL FACTS

Snails prefer to climb up surfaces. If your snails won't move, try holding the paper at a slant.

Snails are members of the mollusk family which includes clams, oysters, mussels and even octopi.

BORROW SEVERAL SNAILS FOR A MOMENT OR TWO

Place them on a piece of black construction paper, then watch the patterns they leave behind.

Gently touch them as their art takes shape.

Pluck your snails off the paper after several minutes, and let them go home.

Hold the paper up to the sun and enjoy the painting you've helped the snails create.

REPTILIAN REVUE

MATERIALS

Brown grocery bag
Scissors

For a turtle shell: Turn a grocery bag upside down. Cut a hole in the bottom big enough for a child's head to fit through. Then cut armholes in each side of the bag.

AGES

Preschoolers
(Adults construct the shell and kids do the rest.)

REPTILIAN FACTS

Unlike mammals, reptiles hatch from eggs and are cold-blooded. Mammals have a constant body temperature. A reptile's temperature goes up and down depending on how warm or cold the environment is.

Turtle or tortoise? Some turtles can live on land and some can live in water. All tortoises live on land.

WHAT IS A REPTILE?

Imagine you are an animal with no fur or hair.

Instead, a shield of scales is what you wear.

Pretend you have short legs, or maybe no legs at all.

Become a reptile so you can slither and crawl.

TURTLE TUCK

Change into a turtle.

Pull on a paper bag shell and slowly crawl across the ground.

Tuck your head and arms into the bag.

Feel what it is like to hide and sleep inside a shell.

Don't you feel safe?

SNAKE SLITHER

Flick your tongue in and out and hiss like a snake.

Hold your arms next to your sides and pretend to slither through the grass on your belly.

Coil up as tight as you can.

Now uncurl and stretch out as far as you can.

LIZARD PUSH-UPS

Imagine you're a lizard.

Wait on a warm rock for a yummy insect to fly by.

Lie on your belly and do push-ups!

Push your arms and the top half of your body up and down, up and down.

You're letting other lizards know that this is your rock!

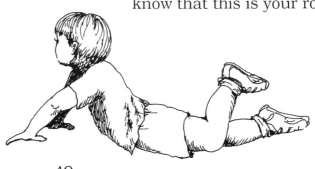

ANIMAL SIGNS AND FINDS

AGES

Toddlers and up

Take out a little time

To hunt for animal signs.

If animals themselves are hard to find

Search for trails they've left behind.

Look for:

Tracks in mud or dirt.

Thin paths winding up hills
and around bushes where
animals walk.

Animal poop such as rabbit droppings, coyote scat and birdy splat!

Nibbled grass and leaf tips.

Piles of sticks collected by wood rats.

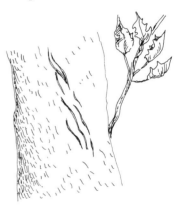

Scratches in tree bark made by climbing animals.

Floating feathers dropped by birds overhead.

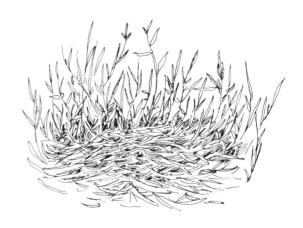

Matted down patches of grass where animals have slept.

ANIMAL HOMES AND HIDEAWAYS

WHERE DO ANIMALS LIVE?

Keep your eyes open for animal homes as you walk and play outdoors.

Animals have all sorts of homes. They have special places to play, places to eat, places to sleep, bathroom places and even places to have babies.

Lie down close to the earth.

You'll find animals hiding above and below you and even to the sides of you.

Many animals like to live in dark, safe places where they can hide from the hot sun or from the cold wind and rain or from other animals that scare them.

Watch for caves, holes and cracks.

These can all be animal homes.

Peek under a rock or piece of wood lying on the ground.

Lots of insects live in the damp protected earth underneath. You might find earwigs, ants, sow bugs, pill bugs, centipedes and beetles.

When you peek behind loose bark, please take care not to pull it off! The animals and nests beneath will not survive if their protective covering is pulled off.

Peer into a flower or inspect a leaf.

Ladybugs, leafhoppers, moths, butterflies, ants and aphids love to hide and feast on tasty plants.

Search for other animal homes.

Some animals live under the water, some even live on top!

Some, like birds, beavers and wood rats, build homes out of leaves, branches and sticks.

Some, like wasps, build homes out of mud.

Spiders spin their homes out of sticky silvery strands made from a liquid that they keep stored inside their bodies.

Turtles carry their shell homes on their backs.

IF YOU LIVED IN THE WILDERNESS, WHAT KIND OF HOME WOULD YOU HAVE?

BECOME A TREE

Become an oak, walnut or sycamore tree
Blow like a seed in the wind
Plant yourself in the earth
Press your roots deep into the ground
Push your little stem up through the soil

Sprout twigs
Spread out your limbs ...
Listen to the birds singing in your branches
Feel a squirrel climbing up your trunk
Rustle your leaves in the wind
Sniff the fresh smell of your flowers
Burst into fruit

Open your arms to welcome summer sunshine
Drop your leaves to welcome fall
Feel the tickle of the winter rain
Start to grow again, *IT'S SPRING*

A TREE IS LIKE ME

MATERIALS

A tree
The tune to Twinkle
  Twinkle Little Star

AGES

Toddlers and up

HURTING TREES

Sometimes people who don't understand a tree will carve words and pictures into its bark. This hurts the tree and opens wounds for bugs and germs to crawl into. If your tree has been hurt, it may need a hug.

HAVE YOU EVER NOTICED HOW MUCH A TREE'S BODY LOOKS LIKE YOUR BODY?

Stand beneath a tree and pick up one of its fallen leaves.

Hold your hand and the leaf out at the same time.

Can you see that a leaf has fingers just like you? A leaf also has veins just like your hands do. (If you can't find veins in your own hands, find them in Mom's or Dad's hands.)

> Sing: My friend tree, my friend tree, leaves on you are like hands on me!
> (Song verses can be repeated.)

Run your hand up and down the tree's trunk. Feel the bark.

Bark protects the inside of a tree and keeps all the tree's food and water inside.

Rub your hand up and down your arm and feel your skin.

Your skin protects your insides too!

> Sing: My friend tree, my friend tree, bark on you is like skin on me!

Lift your arms high above your head and look up into the tree.

What part of the tree do your arms look like?

> Sing: My friend tree, my friend tree, branches on you are like arms on me!

Hold your arms next to your sides with your feet together standing straight and tall.

What is holding you up? Your legs, of course! Just like your legs, a trunk is what holds a tree up.

> Sing: My friend tree, my friend tree, a trunk on you is like legs on me!

Look at your feet. Your feet support your legs and keep you from falling down.

Way down underneath the ground grow a tree's roots. Roots dig into the earth and give a tree the strength it needs to stand.

> Sing: My friend tree, my friend tree, roots on you are like feet on me!

ARE YOU AS BIG AS A TREE?

MATERIALS

A big tree
A seedling
A tape measure

AGES

Toddlers
Preschoolers

MEASURE A TREE IN DIFFERENT WAYS

Take a tape measure and measure a tree's trunk to see how fat it is.

Hold hands if you have friends along and see how many of you it takes to surround a tree.

How big are the tree's leaves?

Are they bigger than your hands?

Is the bark of the tree thick or thin?

Is it thicker than your skin?

Stand tall and raise your arms.

How far up the tree can you reach?

Look for thin new branches.

Look for heavy old branches.

*Can you find a baby tree seedling
growing beneath its mom or dad?*

How big do you think it will grow?

If a tree has lots of sun and water, it will
grow to be very tall. If its earth is dry
and it lives in the shade, it may stay
short and thin.

THE SECRETS OF A TREE

MATERIALS

A tree
Magnifying glasses
Binoculars, real or ...

> Tape two toilet tissue tubes together, punch holes in the top of each side and thread ribbon through for a neck strap.

Stethoscope

AGES

Toddlers
Preschoolers

FIND A SPECIAL TREE AND PRETEND YOU ARE A DETECTIVE

Find which birds, animals and insects live in or visit your tree.

Look on the ground under the tree.

> Nuts or acorns are clues that you have discovered a squirrel's or chipmunk's kitchen cupboard.

Check the tree trunk.

> Are there any holes? Birds peck at the bark looking for insects and insect eggs. Ants like to dig tunnels into the bark. Beetle babies (larvae) dig lacy freeways through the trunk. Bug bathrooms are filled with fras (poo).

Use a magnifying glass and search for insects.

> Moths, beetles, ants and spiders like to nest on the bark.

Search for scratches on the trunk.

Scratches tell that an animal has climbed the tree. Mice, squirrels, chipmunks, raccoons, foxes, lizards and tree frogs all climb trees to look for food. A tree is a restaurant for animals. The menu includes seeds, fruit, berries, eggs, nuts, acorns and insects.

Listen for sounds that come from the tree.

You may hear bees buzz, beetles click, squirrels scold, birds warble or screech and frogs croak.

Listen with a stethoscope for water rushing inside the tree.

Lie on the ground and look up at your tree.

Use binoculars to find birds' nests, beehives and spider webs. Chewed leaves are a sign of snacking insects.

How many creatures have you found in your tree?

GET TO KNOW A SYCAMORE TREE

MATERIALS

A sycamore tree

AGES

Babies and up

SAY HELLO TO A SYCAMORE TREE!

Throw your arms around its trunk and feel its cool, patchy bark.

Rub sycamore leaves on your cheek, arms and legs.

They are soft, fuzzy and shaped like a hand. In the fall, the leaves change color and are fun to crunch or pile up and jump into!

FUZZ TO NEST

Some hummingbirds will gather the soft fuzz off sycamore leaves for their nests. They mix the fuzz with spider webs to create a nest that will expand as their babies grow.

Look for a sycamore's prickly fruit pods.

They grow on stalks in bunches of two's and three's.

Pick off a few pods and stick them to your shirt.

You can wear them like Velcro buttons!

Where else can you attach the pods?

PEEK-A-BOO BARK

MATERIALS

Sycamore tree bark

AGES

Babies and up

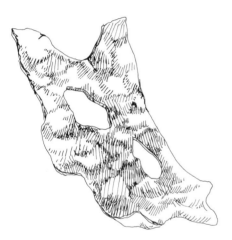

PARENT TIP

A simple game of peek-a-boo can delight babies and toddlers too young to make masks. Parents can hide then peek out from behind a patch of bark. If their baby seems comfortable, they can help her do the same.

BARK MASKS

Turn a patch of tree bark into a magical mask.

Search for bark that has peeled off of a sycamore tree.

Can you find bark in different sizes and shapes as you skip around the tree?

Notice that peeled sycamore bark is thin and smooth and often full of "peek holes" that look like Swiss cheese!

Hold a piece of bark up to your face and peek through the holes.

You have just created a sycamore mask!

What do you think you look like behind that bark?

An owl? A lizard? An elf?

Think of all the masks you have at your feet as you stand under this tree.

NATURE'S PUZZLE

Pretend your mask is now a huge puzzle piece.

Find a "bald" spot on the tree where your piece will fit.

You have made a giant natural puzzle.

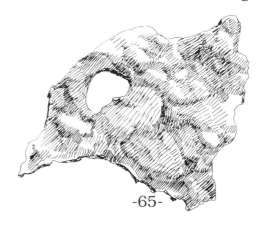

MEET A LEAF

MATERIALS

Crayons
Paper bag
Leaves

AGES

Toddlers
Preschoolers

LEAF MATCHING

Collect a variety of leaves, two of each kind, in a paper bag.

Take a closer look at each leaf you have found.

Help your child describe it. What tree did it come from? Is it long or short? Is it narrow or wide? Is it smooth or furry? What color is it? Is it shaped like your hand?

Together, find each leaf's match in your collection.

RETURN EVERYTHING

Leaves and bark are used as food and shelter by insects and animals. Dead plants are used as nutrients to foster new growth. It is important to return everything that you pick up so it can be used again.

Make a crayon rubbing.

Place a leaf between two
pieces of paper and rub a
crayon over it. You will have
a lovely memory of your
favorite leaves!

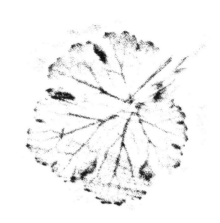

Return the leaves to their homes.

Help your child place the
leaves in the area where you
found them. You will be
amazed at your child's
memory!

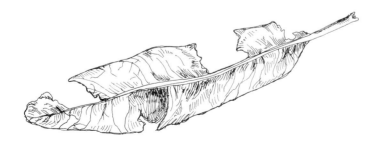

ACORNS ACORNS ACORNS

MATERIALS

Acorns

AGES

Toddlers
Preschoolers

SAFETY TIP

When looking at animal homes be careful not to put hands or fingers into the holes.

WHO ELSE USED ACORNS ?

Acorns were an important and favorite food of most North American Indians. The acorns were mashed then soaked until they tasted sweet. The nut meat was dried and ground into a high-protein meal for bread. Acorns need to be soaked many times to eliminate toxic tannins.

HELP THE SQUIRRELS AND BIRDS GATHER FOOD FOR THE WINTER

Collect acorns by looking under oak trees or by rummaging through piles of oak leaves.

Search for holes in the ground or in trees and logs.

These holes are homes for squirrels, chipmunks, birds and other animals that love to eat acorns.

Drop piles of acorns next to these homes so animals can easily find them.

Your animal friends will store these acorns and eat them during winter when berries and other foods are hard to find.

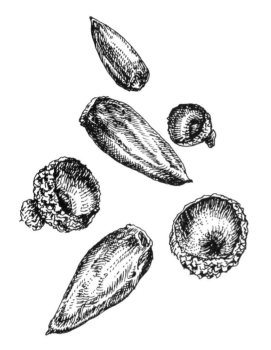

Look for acorn hats.

Can you find any acorns that have lost their hats?

Acorns have a cap on the stem end that looks like a hat.

The caps often fall off and can be found scattered on the ground.

See how many hats you can place back on the acorns.

Try to place an acorn hat on your own head!

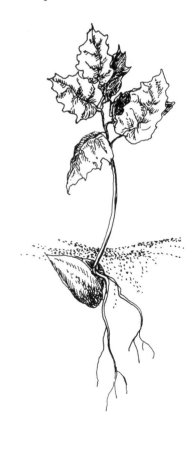

Plant an acorn.

The acorn is the seed of the oak tree. If you cover your acorn with earth it might grow into a beautiful oak tree.

GRASS PLAY

MATERIALS

Tall, soft, swaying
  grasses, commonly
  found along trail
  edges
Short, thin, green
  grass blades

AGES

Babies and up
  for tickle grass
Preschoolers and up
  for whistle grass

STOP TO PLAY WITH GRASSES ALONG THE TRAIL

WHISTLE GRASS

Pluck a short green grass blade and put it between your thumbs.

Take a deep breath and blow through your thumbs to make a whistling noise.

TICKLE GRASS

Bend a tall grass stem toward your face. Tickle your chin, your cheeks, your arms and your knees with the feathery grass tips.

Tickle a friend.

BLOSSOMS TO BUBBLES

MATERIALS

Spray bottle filled with
 water
Ceanothus flowers
 (California lilac)

AGES

Babies and up

Ceanothus blooms from February to May. The flower clusters range from white to light purple. They have a delicate lilac fragrance which is why they are also called California lilac.

FLOWERS MAKE SOAP

Pick a flower cluster from a Ceanothus bush.

Place it in your hand and spray it with water.

Rub your hands together.

You will soon notice a soapy feeling. Look! You have just made sweet-smelling soapsuds like Indians did long ago.

Enjoy the suds!

THIRSTY FRIENDS

Instead of picking flowers, water the plants on your way home.

Use your spray bottle to say hello to plants and trees.

Our plant friends need water too.

Of course, plants usually get their water from rain, morning dew and streams. They store their water inside their trunks, stalks, roots and leaves.

The plants thank you for being so generous.

It is wonderful to share water with our thirsty friends.

TRAIL FARMERS

MATERIALS

Seeds

AGES

Toddlers
Preschoolers

HELP A SEED PLANT ITSELF

Find a dandelion tuft and give it a puff.

Watch its furry seeds float through the air.

Dandelions can drift far from home with the help of the wind or a passing animal friend. This is how dandelions replant themselves.

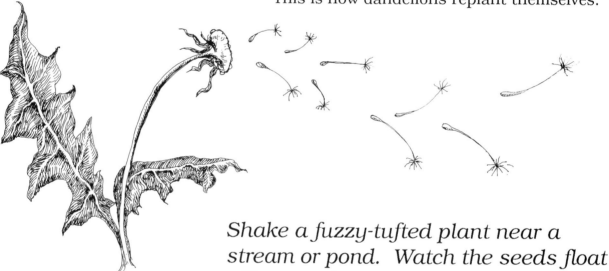

Shake a fuzzy-tufted plant near a stream or pond. Watch the seeds float off to new homes.

MADE TO TRAVEL

Seeds need to travel away from parent plants so they don't get overcrowded. They need the wind and animals to help them move. Squirrels and woodpeckers are famous animal farmers because they love to hide seeds by burying them or storing them for winter food.

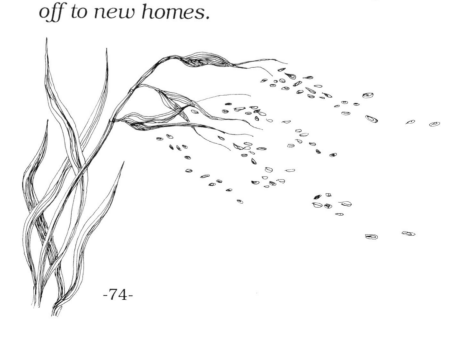

-74-

LOOK FOR HITCHHIKING SEEDS

Check your clothes, especially shoe-laces and socks, for seeds that have hopped onto you for a free ride.

Some seeds travel by hooking themselves onto animal fur and little hikers' socks. They loosen and mix with soil when the animal lies down for a rest or returns to its home.

Catch a fuzzy seed and connect it to your shirt.

Can you give it a ride to a new home?

FIND A SEED POD

Dig a hole.

Drop your seed into the hole and cover it with earth.

YOU ARE NOW A TRAIL FARMER!

TIDEPOOLS IN PAILS

MATERIALS

Saltwater, rocks, seaweed, shells, sand, toy fish and a clear plastic container

AGES

Toddlers
Preschoolers

TINY TIDEPOOLS

Fill a clear plastic container with saltwater, then drop in several toy fish.

Pretend that your bobbing fish are real, and decide what you can add to the container to help them survive.

Collect seaweed, rocks, shells and sand for the fish, then place your goodies into the container.

Touch and play with the objects in your completed tidepool.

Talk about where your fish are hiding and about what they are eating.

Imagine your container is a lagoon for baby fish.

FRAGILE TIDEPOOLS

Tidepool animals are very fragile and few in number. We must take great care when we visit their tidepool homes. Please be sure not to use any live tidepool critters in your container!

You can sing this song

to the tune of
"If You're Happy and You Know It."

I'm a little baby fish in the lagoon.

I'm a little baby fish in the lagoon.

As the pelicans fly past,

I hide in the tall grass.

I'm a little baby fish in the lagoon.

BABY BEACHCOMBERS

MATERIALS

Paper bags
Keen eyes

AGES

Toddlers
Preschoolers

HELP THE BIRDS AND OTHER BEACH ANIMALS CLEAN UP THEIR HOME

With paper bag in hand, collect all the trash that litters your path. (Careful if your feet are bare.)

Keep an eager eye open for styrofoams, plastics, metals and glass. These are especially hazardous to our beach-dwelling friends.

Strike up a conversation about the dangers of trash on the sand and in the water.

Glass and metals cut; plastics and fishing line tangle fragile legs and wings; styrofoam and plastic bags, if accidentally swallowed, cause stomachaches or serious illness—even choking.

Listen and sing with the seabirds as they thank you for making their home safe and clean.

Clean-Up Song

Pickin' up trash and put it in a trash sack
Pickin' up trash and put it in a trash sack
Pickin' up trash and put it in a trash sack
Throwing it away will make the beaches* safe and clean

*the mountains
*the canyons

This little song/chant can be used anywhere you might be walking.

BEACH PLAY

MATERIALS

Seaweed

AGES

Toddlers
Preschoolers

SEA COSTUMES

Dress up in a long piece of seaweed.

Tie it around your waist like a hula skirt or toss it over your shoulders like a Hawaiian lei.

Make up a sea dance to go along with your new costume.

BECOME A BEACH BIRD

Circle and dive like a seagull.

Run back and forth like a sanderling.

Stand on one leg like a sandpiper.

Waddle from side to side like a duck.

Can you find any other birds to imitate?

BEACH TRACKS

Look for footprints and animal tracks in the sand.

Follow the prints and see if you can figure out who or what has made them.

Do they belong to a bird, a dog, a sand crab or a person?

Make your own footprint next to someone else's.

Which footprint is bigger?

CASTLES IN THE SAND

MATERIALS

Sand

AGES

Toddlers
Preschoolers

Walk along the beach and collect interesting rocks, shells, feathers, seaweed and seagrass in a bucket.

Build a big mountain-like sand castle.

Decorate your castle with all the things that you found along the beach.

Enjoy your new kingdom ...

You can leave it behind knowing that birds
and sandcrabs will play in it too.

As you fall asleep at night, think how the
waves are wearing your castle down and
spreading your decorations along the beach
for other people to discover and enjoy
tomorrow.

P O N D   S C O O P

MATERIALS

A pond or stream
Aquatic net with long
   handle
Plastic bags

AGES

Toddlers
Preschoolers

STREAMS AND PONDS CAN OFFER AN EXCITING PARADE OF BUGS AND ANIMALS

The trick is finding water friends without falling in!

Use an aquatic net with a long handle to scoop up back swimmers, dragonfly and damselfly nymphs, pollywogs or even a predacious water beetle.

If you are real quick, you just might catch a crayfish or frog!

Place your newly caught friends in a plastic bag filled with pond water.

CAUTION!

Water beetles have a tendency to bite if handled. It is best to take care and observe them through plastic bags instead of on a hand!

Pond and stream banks are muddy and slippery. Adults need to hold on to children near the water.

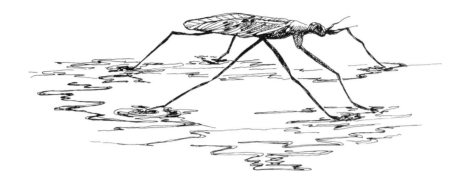

Watch how they swim. Do they stay under or on top of the water? Do they have fins, feet or tails?

You might have moved a rock or log in the process of finding a water buddy. Remember, this rock or log is home for many animals and needs to be left just as it was found.

Gently return water friends to their homes when your short visit is over.

MOUNTAINS TO SAND

This song or chant is especially fun to sing when you're near mountains, walking along a streambed or strolling along a beach.

Mountains getting washed away
Mountains getting older
Mountains getting washed away
And turning into boulders

Boulders getting washed away
Boulders getting knocks
Boulders rolling down the hill
And turning into rocks

Rocks are getting churned around
Isn't it incredible?
Rocks are washing down the stream
And turning into pebbles

Pebbles getting smaller now
It's hard to understand
As time flows by my pebbles
They will finally turn to sand!

MOUNTAINS

Look up at a mountain or hill and become the mountain by raising your arms above your head.

BOULDERS

Become a boulder by making a circle with your arms out in front of you. Turn around in a circle like you're rolling down a hill.

ROCKS

Hug yourself and move around like you're a rock tumbling in a stream.

SAND

Pick up a handful of sand and let it slip out between your fingers.

MAKE A VOLCANO

MATERIALS

2 tbs baking soda
2 tbs clear dish soap
   colored with orange
   food coloring
1/4 cup white vinegar
Earth
Small jar or container

AGES

Adult help required

All ages can either
   watch or help the
   adults

WATCH A VOLCANO ERUPT

Build up a mountain of earth around a small jar or container.

For the most dramatic effect the container should be larger around the bottom than around the top.

The opening of your jar should form a hole or crater in the middle of your mountain.

Add baking soda and then the dish soap mixture into the crater.

WHAT IS A VOLCANO?

Volcanos are formed when rock underneath the earth becomes so hot it melts. The melted rock, called lava, finds a weak spot or opening in the earth's crust and breaks through. The melted rock flows up through the weak spot and keeps piling until an entire mountain is formed. Gases get trapped inside the rock, and eventually explode—causing a volcanic eruption.

Hand your child the vinegar and have her pour it into the crater to start "an eruption."

Stand back and watch your volcano bubble as the imaginary lava flows over and down the sides of your mountain.

S O R T - A - R O C K

MATERIALS

Empty egg cartons
  shaded with color
Spray bottle filled with
  water
Rocks

AGES

Toddlers
Preschoolers

If a child is too young for color matching, she will have fun putting rocks into the carton and spilling them out again.

DISCOVER THE MANY COLORS IN ROCKS

Start by coloring the bottoms of egg carton cups with different shades of green, brown, black, white, gray, red and purple.

Gather up a variety of rocks from a trail or from your backyard.

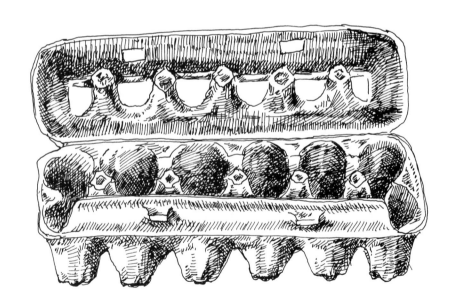

WHY DO ROCKS HAVE COLORS?

Rocks are made up of minerals. If you see oranges and reds there could be iron in your rock. Greens could mean serpentine or green jasper are present in your rock. Clear glassy-looking bits of white, gray, pink and yellow are often quartz. Solid pinks, peaches and reds are often feldspar.

Spray rocks with water to make their colors stand out.

Pick out one rock at a time and see if its color comes close to any of the shades in your egg carton.

Plop your rock into the closest matching carton cup.

Remember to leave the rocks behind when the matching game is through.

ROCK MUSIC

MATERIALS

Empty container with
  lid
Rocks

AGES

Toddlers
Preschoolers

ROCK CONCERT

Fill an empty unbreakable container with a number of fun-looking rocks. Fit the container with a tight lid. You have created a rock drum.

Sit back and listen as you shake and play your new instrument.

When the concert is over and it is time to move on, pour the rocks out for the next hiker to enjoy.

ROCK PITCH

The more heat and pressure a rock has been under during its formation, the harder it is and the higher pitch it will make when tapped against another rock.

RHYTHM ROCKS

*Find two rocks, one for each hand.
Practice tapping them together to see
what sound they make. Do they
make a high clink, or a low thud?
Sing or chant the following along with
your rock sound!*

Clink, clink, stop
Clink, clink, shhh
Clink them to the side and the other side too
Clink, clink, stop
Clink, clink, shhh
Clink them way up high, then lay them on
your shoes

SAND SLIDES

MATERIALS

Sand
3x5 index cards
Clear tape
Magnifier
Scissors or hole punch

AGES

Toddlers
Preschoolers
(Adults construct the slide and kids do the rest.)

CREATE A SAND SCAN SLIDE

Punch or cut out several small holes in a 3x5 index card.

Cover the underside of each hole with clear sticky tape.

Press your "slide" into the sand, sticky side down, to pick up several small patches of sand.

Credit for this idea goes to our friend and resource, Jean Dillingham.

Hold a magnifying glass close to your slide, and watch the sand become bigger.

Notice that sand is made up of millions of sand grains which are teeny tiny bits of rock. Sometimes bits of shell from sea animals are mixed in with the sand grains.

How many colors and shapes can you find in the sand grains?

Close your eyes and picture each grain of sand being at one time part of a huge rock or mountain.

ME AND MY SHADOW

MATERIALS

A sunny day

AGES

Toddlers
Preschoolers

WAIT FOR A SUNNY DAY

Dance around and spot your shadow.

Is it big, small or hardly there at all?

Play a game of follow-the-leader with your shadow.

Run, jump, tiptoe, sit, walk, then turn around.

Can you play hide-and-seek with your shadow, or does it follow too close?

See how big and strong you can make your shadow look.

Have a friend trace that giant shadow in the dirt with a finger.

Jump into a shady spot under a tree and enjoy the coolness.

Now you're standing in the tree's shadow!

Did your shadow follow you into the tree's shade or did it disappear?

Step back into the sun and find something your shadow can protect from the heat.

Flowers and bugs like shade too.

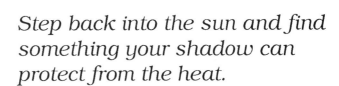

RAINY DAYS

MATERIALS

A rainy day

AGES

Babies and up

AN EXCITING TIME TO BE OUTSIDE IS DURING A LIGHT DRIZZLE OR SEVERAL HOURS AFTER A HARD RAIN

Pull on some rubber boots so you can jump into puddles.

Step outside into the fresh, clean air.

Take a deep breath.

What do you smell? Does the earth smell sweet and damp? What do the rocks, trees and flowers smell like?

Open your eyes and see the color around you. Look how green the plants are and how brown the earth is.

Everything around you has just had a shower and is squeaky clean!

Can you find a spider web sparkling with
water drops?

Look for animal tracks in the soft, damp
ground. Try to make your own tracks.

Listen to the drip, dripping of water falling
off leaves, branches and rooftops.

Stand under a tree and shake one of its
branches. Feel and taste the raindrops fall
onto your face and tongue.

Close your eyes and enjoy how good the
rain makes both you and the earth feel!

WINDY DAYS

MATERIALS

A windy day
A dandelion, a leaf or
a blade of grass

AGES

Toddlers
Preschoolers

WAIT FOR A WINDY DAY

Feel the wind blow through your hair and against your skin.

Does the wind feel warm or cool?

Is it a strong gust, or a gentle breeze?

Listen to the wind whistle through the plants, grass and trees.

Watch it rustle leaves and sway branches.

How does it sound?

Inhale the wind.

Is it carrying the fragrance of spring, of flowers, of sage or of the damp earth after a rain?

Is it carrying the salty scent of the ocean or the warm smell of summer?

Look for pollen, seeds and leaves that the wind is transporting through the air around you.

Pretend you are the wind.

Blow on a dandelion, a blade of grass or a leaf. Blow gently, then as hard as you can.

Now pretend the wind is blowing you!

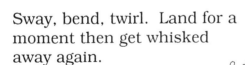

Sway, bend, twirl. Land for a moment then get whisked away again.

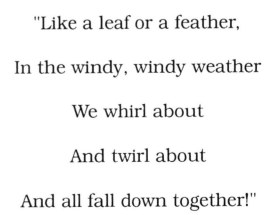

"Like a leaf or a feather,

In the windy, windy weather

We whirl about

And twirl about

And all fall down together!"

TRAIL MAP

MATERIALS

Paper
Crayon, pencil or pen

AGES

Preschoolers
(may need parental
help)

DRAW A PICTURE OF YOUR FAVORITE TRAIL

Begin by making a dot or an X on a sheet of paper to show where your trail or path begins.

Now draw a line from the X to the other side of the page.

This line will be the trail.

Decide, as you walk along, what areas or objects you want to draw along the line of your picture map.

Can you find a hollow tree, a stream, a waterfall, a big, colorful rock, a deer trail or a cave?

Stop when you find something that interests you!

Look and enjoy, then sit down and draw your special discovery along the trail line.

You can name these special stopping points too. Some imaginary names could be Elephant Rock, Rainbow Falls, Mustard Meadows, Laughing Cave or Mouse House Tree.

At the end of the trail, hold out your map and remember all the sights you enjoyed along your walk.

Can you follow your picture map and find these special spots again on your way back?

Keep your picture maps!

Next time you visit this trail, take the map with you. See if anything that is on your map has changed. Did a favorite tree grow new leaves? Is there a new animal hole along your path? Are there different flowers blooming in the meadow?

TREASURE HUNT

MATERIALS

Paper bag
Rocks, seeds, feathers,
   leaves, etc.

AGES

Toddlers
Preschoolers

FILL A PAPER BAG WITH TRAIL TREASURES

Gather up a collection of natural treasures as you walk along the trail.

Rocks, seeds, galls, acorns, feathers, leaves and bark make wonderful finds.

Pick up nature's "fun to touch and hold" objects like smooth, cool pebbles, fuzzy dandelions, prickly pods and velvety leaves.

WHAT IS A GALL?

A gall is an odd-looking insect home. Triggered by certain insects, a plant will build a round-shaped, food-filled shelter. This shelter, or gall, grows around an insect's eggs and protects and feeds the insect larvae until they are ready to chew through to face the world. Galls can be found in many sizes, shapes and colors. They can be tiny or as big as an apple.

Peer into your bag when you've finished collecting and pick out a single treasure that interests you most.

Can you name what it is?

Begin a game of seek-and-match.

Search the ground for a partner to your treasure. If you are holding a leaf, can you find another leaf that looks almost the same? If you are holding a pod or seed, can you find any more along the path?

Place your treasure back in the bag when your matching is through.

Shutting eyes tight, reach into the bag and guess what objects you are holding or feeling. Can you name them all?

Return your treasures when it's time to go on.

Part of the fun is remembering where you found them!

MAKING MEMORIES

MATERIALS

A handkerchief or
   piece of cloth
Small natural object
Eyes and ears

AGES

Preschoolers and up

MAKE A PICTURE WITH YOUR MEMORY

Spread a cloth or handkerchief out on the ground.

This will be your picture frame.

Pick up a small natural delight that you find nearby, like a flower, rock, leaf or pod.

Drop your find onto the cloth.

Can you tell a friend or parent about your treasure? Tell him or her what it looks like. Is it sharp or soft? Does it have many colors? Is it round or square or bumpy?

Close both eyes tight and try to see a picture of your discovery.

You have to use your memory!

As you walk home, stop, close your eyes and try to see your picture again.

Can you still make the picture as you fall asleep tonight?

TAKE HOME A SOUND WITH YOUR MEMORY

Your memory can turn your ears into a tape recorder.

Listen carefully to sounds like bird calls and stream gurgles.

You can walk away and use your memory to hear the sounds again and again.

Pick out a sound in nature.

Is the sound high or low? Can you hum along? Is it loud or soft?

As you walk home, try to keep bringing the sound back into your ears.

MOTHER NATURE'S RECYCLING HELPERS

MATERIALS

A pile of leaves, a dead log or a piece of bark

AGES

Toddlers
Preschoolers

CAUTION

Some mushrooms can be very poisonous. Make sure that children keep hands and mouths away from all mushrooms.

WATCH MOTHER NATURE RECYCLE

Find a leaf, a log or a piece of bark that Mother Nature has recycled.

For millions of years, Mother Nature has been recycling or reusing what she makes and grows.

When a flower dies or a leaf falls from a tree, Mother Nature never thinks of throwing them into a trash can! Instead she has special helpers who will turn this flower and leaf into food for other living things.

WHO ARE THESE SPECIAL HELPERS?

Well, they are Fungus, Bacteria and Insects ... the FBI!

Bacteria are little critters much too small to be seen, but they are busy everywhere, turning dead plants and animals back into nourishing soil.

A fungus is like a plant with no stem, leaf or flower.

A MUSHROOM IS A FUNGUS!

See if you can find a dead log or piece of bark surrounded by mushrooms.

These mushrooms are working hard to turn this dead bark back into earth.

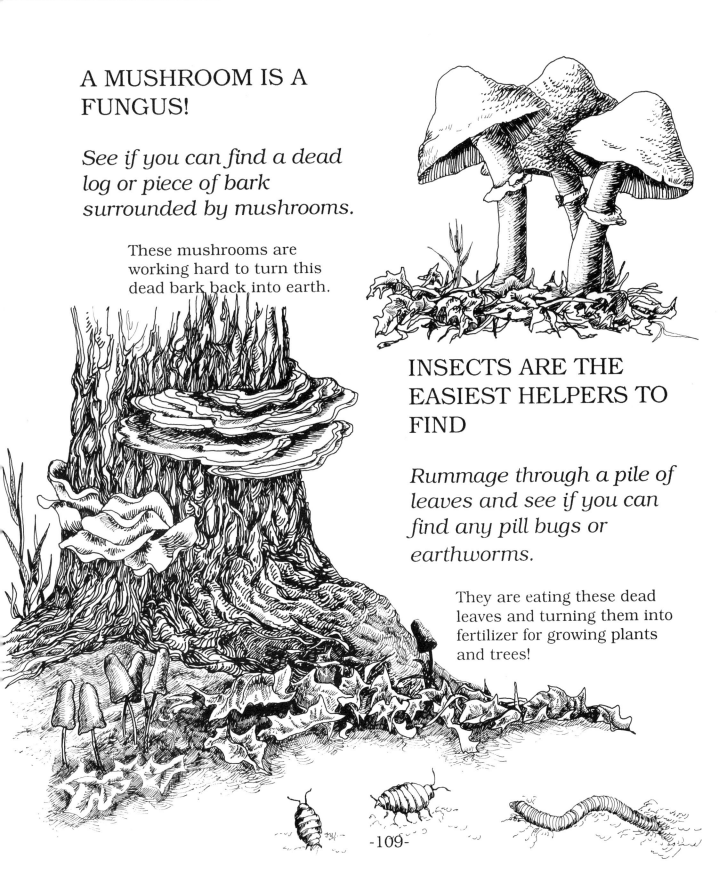

INSECTS ARE THE EASIEST HELPERS TO FIND

Rummage through a pile of leaves and see if you can find any pill bugs or earthworms.

They are eating these dead leaves and turning them into fertilizer for growing plants and trees!

SUBJECT INDEX

AGE-APPROPRIATE INDEX

with help

Why this book was written ...

... because each drop of earth, each grain of sand, each wandering ant, each sprouting seed deserves our attention, wonder, amazement and curiosity.

... because every child deserves to step beyond his or her doorstep and spot a grazing rabbit.

... because plastic is a mono-textured, color-limited, nonscented material and every child deserves to smell, hear, touch and explore the rich and varied sensations of nature.

... because nature is the perfect, free playground in which to form timeless family bonds.

... because developing an interest in the antics and transformations of our animal and plant friends is a gateway to lifelong pleasures.

... because we believe that developing a familiarity with and an appreciation and respect for our wildlife and parklands during the earliest years is the key to the preservation of our Earth.